COME, HOLY SPIRIT

Illustrated by Lyn Ellis

Kevin
Mayhew

First Published in 1993 by
KEVIN MAYHEW LTD
Rattlesden
Bury St Edmunds
Suffolk   IP30 0SZ

ISBN 0 86209 411 9

Front cover: *A still life of lilies and roses*
by Mary Margetts (*d.* 1886).
Reproduced by kind permission of the
Bourne Gallery/Fine Art Photographic
Library Ltd, London.

Printed in Hong Kong

Contents

	Page
THE GRACE OF GOD	7
Trust the past	8
You did not choose	9
When the day of Pentecost	10
The Advocate	11
Eternal God	12
Spirit of Jesus	13
Do not be afraid	14
Jesus is pleased	15
Blessed be the God	16
Deep within them	18
The Father watches	19
Lord Jesus Christ	20
I shall ask	21
God has not promised	22

THE FELLOWSHIP AND BLESSING
OF THE CHURCH   23
   All who believed   24
   May our loving   25
   Lord Jesus, by this . . .   26
   May his love   27
   The cup of blessing   28
   Many grains   29
   Jesus said to them   30
   Lord Jesus, the bread . . .   31
   For I received   32
   May the God of peace   34

FAITH AND COMMITMENT   35
   Take time   36
   Blessed are the poor . . .   38
   The spirit of the Lord   40
   God grant me   41
   Lord, make us   42
   The fruit of the Spirit   43
   Lord, I know you   44
   Live within my love   45
   Lord Jesus, I give you   46
   Go therefore   48

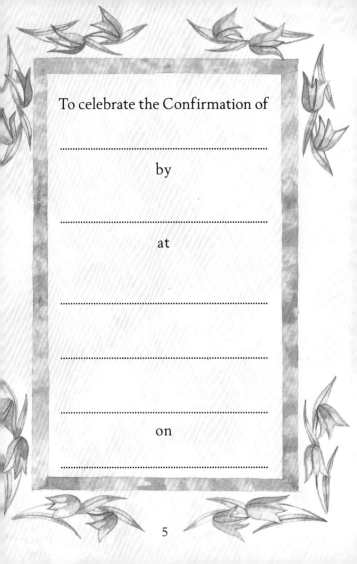

To celebrate the Confirmation of

....

by

....

at

....

....

....

on

....

*Those who love you share the joy
of this special day of days
and pray the Lord will lead you
in the goodness of his ways.
May you follow his direction
and his will in all you do.
May you find his grace sufficient
and his blessings many, too.*

The
Grace of God

Trust the past
to the mercy of God,
the present to his love,
the future to
his providence.

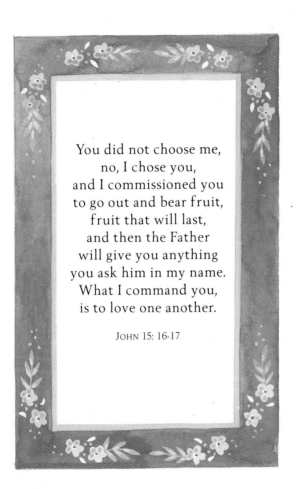

You did not choose me,
no, I chose you,
and I commissioned you
to go out and bear fruit,
fruit that will last,
and then the Father
will give you anything
you ask him in my name.
What I command you,
is to love one another.

JOHN 15: 16-17

When the day
of Pentecost had come,
they were all together
in one place.
And suddenly from heaven
there came a sound
like the rush
of a violent wind,
and it filled
the entire house where
they were sitting.
Divided tongues, as of fire,
appeared among them,
and a tongue rested
on each of them.

ACTS 2: 1-4

The Advocate, the Holy Spirit,
whom the Father will send
in my name,
will teach you everything
and remind you of all
I have said to you.

JOHN 14: 25-26

Eternal God,
you have declared in Christ
the completion of
your purpose of love.
May we live by faith,
walk in hope,
and be renewed in love,
until the world
reflects your glory,
and you are all in all.
Even so; come, Lord Jesus.
Amen.

Spirit of Jesus,
wind, water, fire, come.
Spirit of Jesus,
God's anointing, come.
Spirit of Jesus,
our consoler, come.
Spirit of Jesus,
loving heart of God, come.
Spirit of Jesus,
Dove of Divine Peace, come.
Spirit of Jesus,
first fruits of the glory, come.
Spirit of Jesus,
Breath of the world's
resurrection, come.
Come, Holy Spirit,
my friend, my life.

Do not be afraid,
for I have redeemed you.
I have called you by your name;
you are mine.
When you walk through
the waters, I'll be with you;
You will never sink
beneath the waves.
When the fear
of loneliness is looming,
then remember I am at your side.
You are precious in my eyes,
and honoured, and I love you.

BASED ON ISAIAH 43:1-5

Jesus is pleased to come to us
as the truth to be told
and the life to be lived,
as the light to be lighted
and the love to be loved,
as the joy to be given
and the peace to be spread.

MOTHER TERESA

Blessed be the God
and Father of our Lord Jesus Christ,
who has blessed us in Christ
with every spiritual blessing
in the heavenly places,
just as he chose us in Christ
before the foundation
of the world
to be holy and blameless
before him in love.
He destined us for adoption
as his children
through Jesus Christ,

according to the good
pleasure of his will.
In him you also,
when you had heard
the word of truth,
the gospel of your salvation,
and had believed in him,
were marked with the seal
of the promised Holy Spirit;
this is the pledge of
our inheritance toward
redemption as God's own people,
to the praise of his glory.

EPHESIANS 1:3-5,13-14

Deep within them
I will plant my Law,
writing it on their hearts.
Then I will be their God
and they shall be my people.
There will be no further need
for neighbour to try
to teach neighbour,
or brother to say to brother,
'Learn to know the Lord!'
No, they will all know me,
the least no less
than the greatest –
it is the Lord who speaks –
since I will forgive
their iniquity and never
call their sin to mind.

JEREMIAH 31:33-34

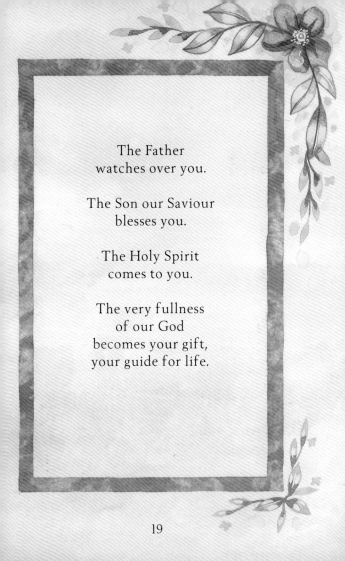

The Father
watches over you.

The Son our Saviour
blesses you.

The Holy Spirit
comes to you.

The very fullness
of our God
becomes your gift,
your guide for life.

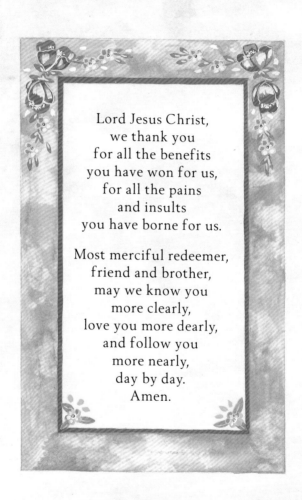

Lord Jesus Christ,
we thank you
for all the benefits
you have won for us,
for all the pains
and insults
you have borne for us.

Most merciful redeemer,
friend and brother,
may we know you
more clearly,
love you more dearly,
and follow you
more nearly,
day by day.
Amen.

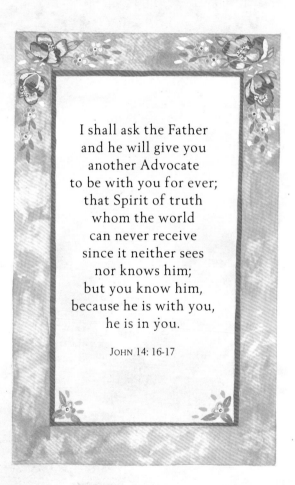

I shall ask the Father
and he will give you
another Advocate
to be with you for ever;
that Spirit of truth
whom the world
can never receive
since it neither sees
nor knows him;
but you know him,
because he is with you,
he is in you.

JOHN 14: 16-17

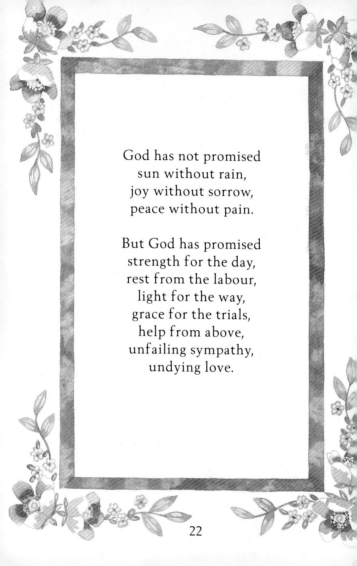

God has not promised
sun without rain,
joy without sorrow,
peace without pain.

But God has promised
strength for the day,
rest from the labour,
light for the way,
grace for the trials,
help from above,
unfailing sympathy,
undying love.

The Fellowship and Blessing of The Church

All who believed
were together and had
all things in common;
they would sell their
possessions and goods
and distribute the proceeds
to all, as any had need.
Day by day,
as they spent much time
together in the temple,
they broke bread at home
and ate their food
with glad and generous hearts.

Acts 2:44-46

May our loving
heavenly Father
guide and keep you
in his care.
May the blessings
of the Holy Spirit
all be yours to share.
May God's wisdom
be the light that leads
your footsteps every day
and his presence
your companion
as you walk
along life's way.

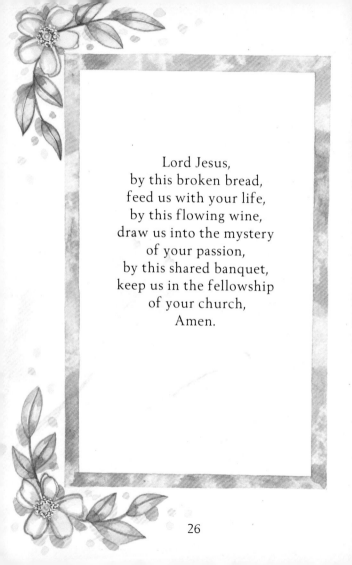

Lord Jesus,
by this broken bread,
feed us with your life,
by this flowing wine,
draw us into the mystery
of your passion,
by this shared banquet,
keep us in the fellowship
of your church,
Amen.

May his love
enfold you.

May his peace
surround you.

May his light
touch you.

The cup of blessing
that we bless,
is it not a sharing
in the blood of Christ?

The bread
that we break,
is it not a sharing
in the body of Christ?

Because there is
one bread,
we who are many
are one body,
for we all partake
of the one bread.

I Corinthians 10:16-17

28

Many grains
come together
into one loaf,
many grapes
come together
into one wine,
so may all creation
come together
into one.
Amen.

Jesus said to them,
'I am the bread of life.
Whoever comes to me
will never be hungry,
and whoever believes in me
will never be thirsty.'

JOHN 6:35

Lord Jesus,
the bread
which is your body
is broken,
the wine
which is your blood
is poured.
Give us grace
to be broken
and poured with you
for the life of your world.
Amen.

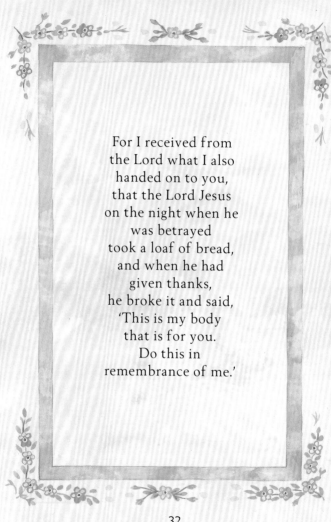

For I received from
the Lord what I also
handed on to you,
that the Lord Jesus
on the night when he
was betrayed
took a loaf of bread,
and when he had
given thanks,
he broke it and said,
'This is my body
that is for you.
Do this in
remembrance of me.'

In the same way
he took the cup
also, after supper, saying,
'This cup is
the new covenant
in my blood.
Do this, as often
as you drink it,
in remembrance of me.'
For as often as you
eat this bread
and drink the cup,
you proclaim the Lord's
death until he comes.

1 CORINTHIANS 11:23-26

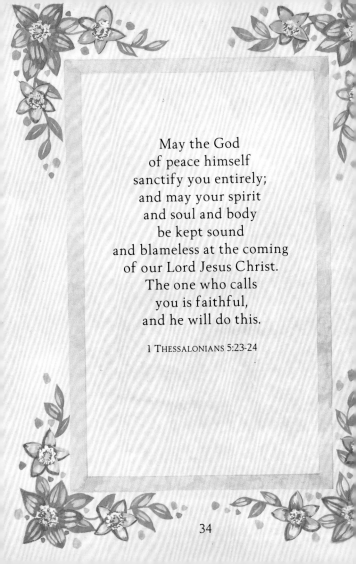

May the God
of peace himself
sanctify you entirely;
and may your spirit
and soul and body
be kept sound
and blameless at the coming
of our Lord Jesus Christ.
The one who calls
you is faithful,
and he will do this.

1 THESSALONIANS 5:23-24

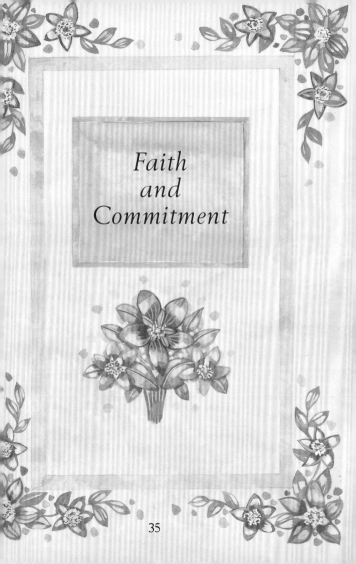

Faith
and
Commitment

Take time to *think* . . .
it is the source of power.
Take time to *play* . . .
it is the secret
of perpetual youth.
Take time to *read* . . .
it is the fountain of wisdom.
Take time to *pray* . . .
it is the greatest
power on earth.
Take time to *love*
and *be loved* . . .
it is a God-given privilege.

Take time to *be friendly* . . .
it is the road to happiness.
Take time to *laugh* . . .
it is the music of the soul.
Take time to *give* . . .
it is too short a day
to be selfish.
Take time to *work* . . .
it is the price of success.
Take time to *do charity* . . .
it is the key to heaven.

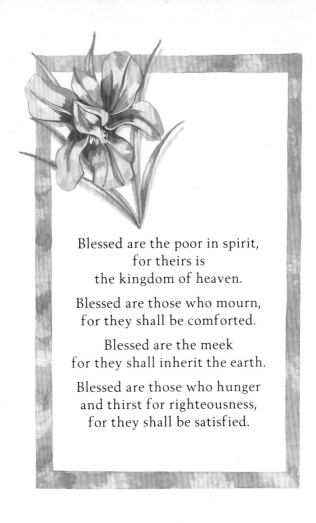

Blessed are the poor in spirit,
for theirs is
the kingdom of heaven.

Blessed are those who mourn,
for they shall be comforted.

Blessed are the meek
for they shall inherit the earth.

Blessed are those who hunger
and thirst for righteousness,
for they shall be satisfied.

Blessed are the merciful
for they shall obtain mercy.

Blessed are the pure in heart
for they shall see God.

Blessed are the peacemakers,
for they shall be called
sons of God.

Blessed are those who are
persecuted for righteousness' sake
for theirs is the kingdom
of heaven.

MATTHEW 5: 3-10

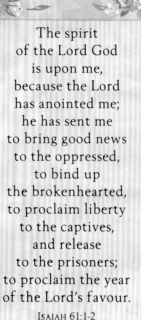

The spirit
of the Lord God
is upon me,
because the Lord
has anointed me;
he has sent me
to bring good news
to the oppressed,
to bind up
the brokenhearted,
to proclaim liberty
to the captives,
and release
to the prisoners;
to proclaim the year
of the Lord's favour.

ISAIAH 61:1-2

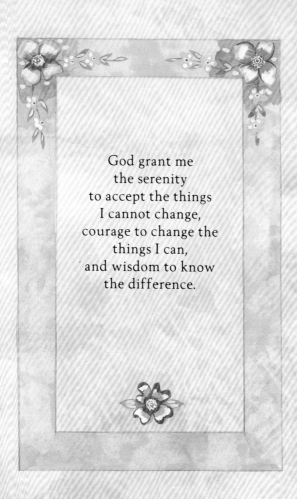

God grant me
the serenity
to accept the things
I cannot change,
courage to change the
things I can,
and wisdom to know
the difference.

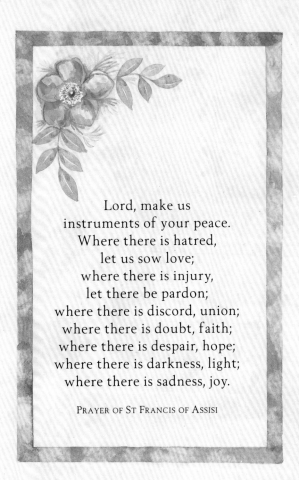

Lord, make us
instruments of your peace.
Where there is hatred,
let us sow love;
where there is injury,
let there be pardon;
where there is discord, union;
where there is doubt, faith;
where there is despair, hope;
where there is darkness, light;
where there is sadness, joy.

PRAYER OF ST FRANCIS OF ASSISI

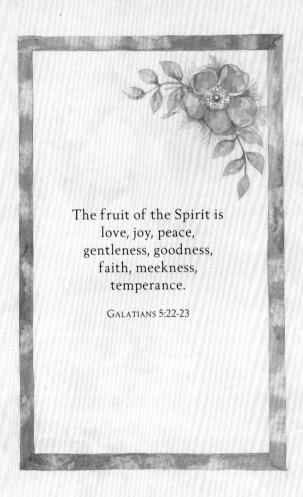

The fruit of the Spirit is
love, joy, peace,
gentleness, goodness,
faith, meekness,
temperance.

Galatians 5:22-23

43

Lord, I know you created me
for a special purpose,
to serve you in a unique way.
You have given me a gift,
and talents,
a certain something
no one else has.
Help me to be a valuable link
in the chain of humanity.
Help me to find peace
and meaning in what I do,
knowing no one else
can be me.

Live within my love.
When you obey me you are
living in my love,
just as I obey my Father
and live in his love.
I have told you this so that
you will be filled with joy.
Yes, your cup of joy
will overflow!

JOHN 15:9-11

Lord, Jesus,
I give you my hands
to do your work.
I give you my feet
to go your way.
I give you my eyes
to see as you do.
I give you my tongue
to speak your words.
I give you my mind
that you may think in me.

I give you my spirit
that you may pray in me.
Above all
I give you my heart
that you may love in me.

I give you my whole self
that you may grow in me,
so that it is you, Lord Jesus,
who live and work
and pray in me.

Go therefore
and make disciples
of all nations,
baptising them
in the name of the Father
and of the Son
and of the Holy Spirit.

<small>MATTHEW 28:19</small>